PHYS...

KINGFISHER

KINGFISHER

Kingfisher Publications Plc
New Penderel House
283–288 High Holborn
London WC1V 7HZ
www.kingfisherpub.com

First published by Kingfisher Plc 2008
10 9 8 7 6 5 4 3 2 1
1TR/1107/SHENS/SCHOY/126.6MA/C

For Kingfisher:
Publisher: Melissa Fairley
Senior Designer: Jane Tassie
Senior Production Controller: Jessamy Oldfield
DTP Manager: Nicky Studdart

For Toucan:
Managing Editor: Ellen Dupont
Text: Dan Green
Editorial Consultant: Giles Sparrow
Consultant: Dr Mike Goldsmith
Dr Mike Goldsmith, an astrophysicist, was formerly head of
Acoustics at the UK's National Physical Laboratory. He is the
author of several science books for children.

Designed and created by Basher www.basherworld.com

Dedicated to Henry Theobalds

A CIP catalogue record for this book is available from the British Library.

ISBN 978 0 7534 1682 2

Printed in Taiwan

CONTENTS

Physics

Introduction

- ✳ Physics is the study of Energy and matter and how they interact
- ✳ The most fundamental and far-reaching of all sciences
- ✳ There's much more to the Universe than meets the eye…

Physics is all about knowing – or trying to find out – what makes the Universe tick. It started out with some naturally nosy people who wanted to know why the things around them did what they did. Nothing has changed today, but over the past few centuries, we've realized that there are whole worlds both bigger and smaller than our human senses can detect.

Physics can be daunting at first, full of facts and formulas, but this book peels back the stuffy layers to show you the main players behind the scenes. You'll meet everyday characters, such as Friction, who slows your bike down, and others, such as the super-fast Neutrinos, who are out of this world. They are a dashing lot, full of pizzazz, and they're all in here waiting for you…

E(instein) = *mc²*

"Everything should be made as simple as possible, but not simpler."   Albert Einstein (1879–1955)

The original absent-minded professor with his mad hair and even madder ideas, Albert Einstein was a superstar scientist who took the world by storm. His revolutionary ideas turned physics – and all of science – on its head.

Physics (and this book) is all about matter and Energy. Matter is the stuff that we can see and feel, and Energy is the stuff that makes it do stuff. Einstein had the genius to see that they are two sides of the same coin and, with a simple bit of maths, he brought the two halves of physics together. His famous equation, $E = mc^2$, says that Energy (E) is equal to Mass (m) times the speed of light squared, and it shows how a jot of Mass can release a tide of Energy. If this wasn't enough, Albert Einstein also had some nifty ideas about how space and time are related. Pretty good for someone who never enjoyed school – there's hope for all of us yet!

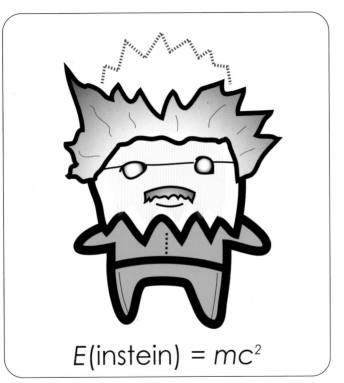

$E(\text{instein}) = mc^2$

Chapter 1
Old School

This robust and gung-ho bunch tell us how things in the everyday world interact with each other. They are big, lumbering lunks who love to knock about together. The Old School all concern matter – the stuff that other stuff is made of – and what happens when forces are put in the mix. Without this lot, there's no way we could even hope to understand our Universe. Even though they are "old school", this gang is showing no sign of slowing down. You could say that these forceful fellows are the ones that really matter!

Mass

Weight

Density

Speed

Acceleration

Force

Inertia

Friction

Gravity

Mass
▥ Old School

* ☀ A measure of the amount of matter in an object
* ☀ Even if Gravity changes, Mass stays the same
* ☀ Intimately connected to Inertia, but measured in kilograms

As someone that gives things their bulk, I'm a solid and dependable kind of guy – a real man of substance. I am the amount of "stuff" an object is made from. Anything, from the tiniest Atom to the most enormous star, has some of me. The only thing in the Universe without me is pure energy, and the waves that carry it.

Want to know how much matter an object has? Check me out! I don't depend on Gravity, so I won't go changing (not like Weight). For scientists, massive doesn't mean huge – dense things cram a lot of Mass into a small space – but usually, the more of me anything has, the bigger it is. Things with loads of me are very attractive. No really! The Universe's most massive objects have their own alluring force of Gravity.

Date of discovery: 1666

● Discoverer: Isaac Newton
● Mass of Earth: 5.976×10^{24} kg
● Mass of Earth's oceans: 1.4×10^{21} kg

Mass

Weight
■ Old School

* Weight is a downward force that depends on Gravity
* He's measured in Newtons, not kilograms
* Don't get him confused with Mass or he'll call in the heavies!

I am the man of the moment! From size-zero models to overweight kids, it's all about "Weight". But actually it's not me that people are obsessed with, it's Mass. Mass tells you how much matter is in an object, whereas I tell you only what force it exerts (what "push" it has).

I have my advantages, though – because I depend on Gravity, I'm dead easy to measure. You can even use me to measure Mass. If something weighs 10 times as much as another thing, it has 10 times as much Mass. Easy! But here's the heavyweight part: things can weigh different amounts on different planets. On the Moon, a dumb-bell would weigh a mere sixth of what it does on Earth because of the lower Gravity there. In space – away from all Gravity – things are weightless.

First weight-driven clock: c.1200

● Weight on Moon: 17% of weight on Earth
● Weight on Mars: 38% of Earth weight
● Weight on Jupiter: 213% of Earth weight

Weight

Density
■ Old School

✳ A way of describing how tightly packed a substance is
✳ The more tightly packed, the denser the substance
✳ Measured in kilograms per cubic metre

Don't be fooled by my name – I'm not dense. I may be thick, but I'm no dummy. A best mate of Mass, I'm the measure of how compact materials are. The more Mass in anything, the denser it is. I'm just the sort of fellow to get you into a tight squeeze, not out of one! Sink or swim, it's all down to me. Less dense things will always rise above denser things. This is why oil slicks float on top of water and balloons filled with lighter-than-air helium sail skywards.

Dense things cram a lot of Mass into a small space, which makes them feel heavy in your hand. Metals are some of the most tightly packed solids – the elements osmium and iridium are the densest on Earth. Black holes are so dense their Gravity even eats up Light.

First density thermometer: 1593

● Density of osmium: 22,610 kg/m³
● Density of iridium: 22,650 kg/m³
● Density of a black hole: 1.8×10^{19} kg/m³

Density

Speed
■ Old School

* Coasts along, covering distance divided by time
* Friction is the only thing that makes Speed lose his cool
* Measured in metres per second

Everybody's in a hurry these days and that makes me a really hot property! Internet connection speed, tight deadlines and speed dating – I'm where it's at. But what's the rush? Chill.

Although I tell you how quickly you can get from A to B, I'm a balanced person and I like things to be paced evenly. If an object has no Force pushing it, it stays still or coasts along at the same unchanging speed. Unlike Acceleration, I'm laid back – you'll get there in the end. No Forces, no sweat!

There are loads of ways to measure me. Pilots use "Mach", which compares a jet's speed to the speed of sound. Sailors use "knots", a ropy old-school method.

First land-speed attempt: 1898

● Speed of light: 299,792,458 m/s
● Land-speed record: 1,223.65 km/h
● Free-fall speed record: 502.1 km/h

Speed

Acceleration
■ Old School

✳ Acceleration is how quickly things pick up Speed
✳ It is not a Force, but you "feel" it as a Force
✳ Measured in metres per second, per second

Forget the need for Speed – I've got what it takes to get you going. I'm what makes things pull away from each other, like cars at the traffic lights. I'm a total adrenaline junkie who likes to live life in the fast lane.

To fire me up, forces have to be unbalanced and I always zip off in the direction of the bigger Force. You can tell when I'm around, because as I overcome Inertia, you feel it pushing you back in your seat. Astronauts feel this as "g-forces" ("g" for Gravity), as they accelerate against the force of Gravity.

The quickest off the mark in the animal kingdom is the cheetah. For speed freaks, drag racers and rockets are the fastest-accelerating man-made machines.

Date of discovery: 1553

● Discoverer: Giambattista Benedetti
● Acceleration of a cheetah: 144 m/s^2
● Acceleration of a drag racer: 2400 m/s^2

Acceleration

Force
■ Old School

* An overpowering bully boy measured in Newtons
* Gangs up with Mass and Acceleration to push things about
* All of this fellow's actions are due to four fundamental forces

I invite you to feel the Force! You can't see me. You can't hold me. But you can *feel* me. You can feel me in the grip of your tyres on the road; when you kick a ball hard and send it flying; if you've ever struggled to lever open a tin of baked beans or reeled around in a country dance. I overcome Inertia to push, pull and twist things around, but I have a tendency to get out of control. When moving things crash, I go haywire and create a mangled wreck.

My golden rule is that for every bit of me produced, there is another, equal bit of me produced in the opposite direction. This simple policy stops your feet from sinking into the floor when you walk. It is also how space rockets travel and why running into a wall is a bad idea!

Date of discovery: 1666

● Discoverer: Isaac Newton
● Fundamental forces: Gravity, Weak Force, Strong Force, Electromagnetism

Force

Inertia
▦ Old School

☀ A two-faced grump measured in Newton-metres
☀ Makes objects refuse to be moved at first…
☀ …then makes them difficult to stop!

I know I can be difficult, stubborn and sluggish, but it's my nature. I am an object's resistance to motion. To get anything to move, you must first overcome me – and the bigger an object, the less inclined I am to budge. People have Inertia too. It's tricky to get them to do anything when they don't want to – and you know how hard it is to get out of bed in the mornings!

But there are two ways for this cookie to crumble and I have a dangerous flipside. When I get going I'm like a runaway train. It's hard for me to stop. In this disguise, I go by the name of momentum. While Inertia is all to do with an object's Mass, momentum is what happens when Mass teams up with Speed. Objects happily pass their momentum to another object when they collide.

Date of discovery: 1666

● Discoverer: Isaac Newton
● Idea first used: Aristotle, 330BCE
● Used to measure Mass in zero gravity

Inertia

Friction
■ Old School

☀ A stick-in-the-mud force who hates all sorts of movement
☀ Caused when two surfaces slide past each other
☀ This over-heated chunk takes orders from Entropy

I'm a fly in the ointment, a spanner in the works and a frequent cause of aggro. My disruptive force makes Energy lose its usefulness, wears out mechanical parts and generates heat in moving things and electrical components. Don't talk to me about that smoothie Speed – I'm hell-bent on slowing him down! I'm also a secret agent for Entropy – the Universe's king of chaos. By generating excess heat, I take useful energy – like Kinetic Energy – out of a system and spread it around.

Things may be a bit of a drag when I'm around, but don't think I'm good for nothing. Without me, the world would be a very slippery place – your shoes wouldn't grip the ground and the brakes on your cars and bikes would be useless. You need me more than you know it!

Earliest use: 1.8 million years ago

● Slipperiest stuff: Near Frictionless Carbon
● Stickiest stuff: a glue made by molluscs
● Drag on a car at 100 km/h: about 280 N

Friction

Gravity
■ Old School

- ☀ The force of attraction between two objects
- ☀ A fundamental force that never quite disappears
- ☀ The Gravity of huge galaxies can actually bend Light

I am a mystical mover and shaker, and my field of operations is the vastness of space. A universal fixer, I hold the Earth together, keep the planets in their orbits and make stars form, as well as more mundane tasks, such as keeping your feet on the ground. I do my work over very long distances, with no strings attached.

I was the first of the four fundamental forces to be found. (We are the forces that do the Universe's work, and keep things ticking over.) I combine with Mass to keep you pinned down and stop you jumping too high. I am the weakest of the four, but you still keep falling for me! Space rockets must use Acceleration to escape me. I power waterwheels, rollercoasters and grandfather clocks – and I'm also pretty essential for skydivers too!

Date of discovery: 1666

- ● Discoverer: Isaac Newton
- ● Range: infinite
- ● Carrier: graviton (unobserved)

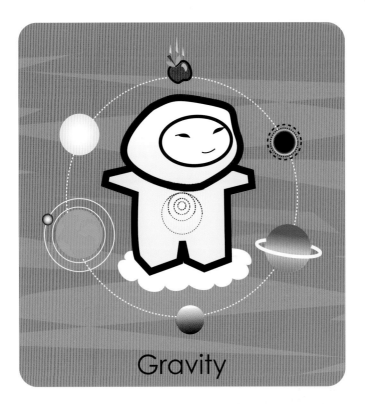

Gravity

Chapter 2
Hot Stuff

If you're in need of a little oomph, look no further! This high-octane group are literally bursting with pep and lust for life. These guys get things done for you and provide the necessary drive to start things moving and growing on Earth. Scientists know an awful lot about how this team interact with each other, but the truth be told, Energy is still mysterious stuff. They're from the other side of the tracks to the matter meatheads of the Old School gang and their high spirits and verve make them an entirely different prospect...

Energy

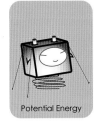

Potential Energy

Kinetic Energy

Entropy

Vacuum

Black Body Radiation

Energy
■ Hot Stuff

✳ Energy is hot stuff that has a burning desire to get things done!
✳ The amount of Energy and Mass in the Universe is constant
✳ Measured in Joules, or calories in food

Mighty and morphing, I exist in many guises and I make the Universe tick. My incredible ability to slide effortlessly between my different forms drives nature and machine alike. I give you get-up-and-go, enable plants to grow and your brain to think; engines turn Potential Energy (fuel) and Kinetic Energy (motion) into power. Humans worship me and start wars over the means to my production, but still waste vast amounts of me every day.

Most of the Energy on Earth comes from the Sun, which gives off more Energy in one second than all the world's most powerful nuclear reactors put out in one year! I am everything there is. Einstein said that even matter – the stuff that you, me and everything else is made of – is just a super-condensed form of me. Neat, huh?

Date of discovery: 1823

● Discoverer: Sadi Carnot
● Energy used in USA per year: 9×10^{19} J
● Power output of Sun: 4×10^{26} J/s

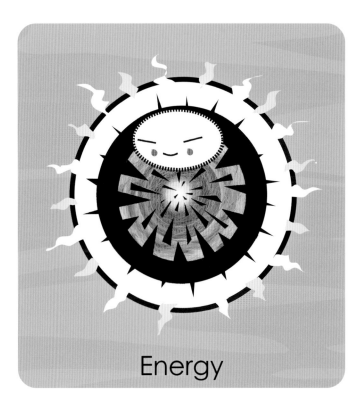

Energy

Potential Energy
■ Hot Stuff

✹ Potential Energy is "Energy on tap"
✹ It is stored Energy, which can be turned into Kinetic Energy
✹ Highly strung and ready to go off, "PE" is measured in Joules

Like a tiger ready to pounce, I'm poised, ready for action and raring to go. I am the Energy in a stretched catapult, a coiled spring, a rollercoaster at the top of a ramp, a chocolate bar and a fully charged battery.

I literally have loads of potential. I am stored Energy that can be converted to other forms. Like money, I'm described by where I am stored. But instead of cash, cheques, gold and jewellery, I come as elastic, gravitational, electrical and chemical Potential Energy. Springs use stored elastic Energy to drive mechanisms such as wind-up watches. Many things are powered by objects falling under Gravity. Batteries power electrical devices and the chemical energy stored in the sugar of a soft drink will have you bouncing off the ceiling!

Date of discovery: 1850s

● Discoverer: William Rankine
● Highest rollercoaster drop: 139 m
● Energy in 100 g of chocolate: 2000 kJ

Potential Energy

Kinetic Energy
■ Hot Stuff

☀ A dynamic character who gives pizzazz to things on the move
☀ Heat is the Kinetic Energy of a substance's molecules
☀ Depends on Mass and Speed, measured in Joules

I am the buzz that speed freaks chase. I'm what happens when Mass gets in motion. I adore Acceleration – as a thing picks up Speed, it gains Kinetic Energy. Skydivers falling out of the sky can almost feel their Potential Energy changing into me by the second as the ground rushes towards them.

I'm used to make electricity and power all kinds of machines. All this gusto can come at a cost, though. I'm the one who kills people in a car crash because I depend on Speed squared – travel twice as fast and you have four times as much of me. I am genuinely hot stuff. The hotter an object gets, the more internal energy its molecules gain and the more they jostle about. This is one of the ways that Entropy decreases my usefulness.

Date of discovery: 1829

● Discoverer: Gaspard-Gustave de Coriolis
● Energy of nuclear bomb: 4×10^{15} J
● Power of hurricane: 1.3×10^{17} J/day

Kinetic Energy

Entropy
▪ Hot Stuff

✴ The measure of disorder in the Universe
✴ A master of disaster and the enemy of all machines
✴ The perfect excuse for never tidying your bedroom!

I am the King of Chaos – a mix-up merchant who makes sure that Energy always changes from useful forms to messed-up, spread-out forms. A renowned troublemaker, I'm the reason why things break and burn out, and I'll get you, too, in the end. Ultimately, I'll cause your body's cells to degrade and stop working properly, and you'll die.

I always increase and I work in one direction only – things NEVER get tidier, unless you put some effort in. Petrol has lots of Potential Energy tied up in its orderly arrangement of Atoms, but when it explodes, this stored Energy is spread out irreversibly. The chaos has increased, so there's more of me. Hooray! In short, I create havoc. This is why it's pointless tidying your room, because the Universe is working against you. Next time, try that as an excuse!

Date of discovery: 1865

● Discoverer: Rudolf Clausius
● Heat that fire-walkers withstand: 650 °C
● Lowest boiling point: –269 °C (helium)

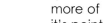

Entropy

37

Vacuum
■ Hot Stuff

☀ An empty void where there is no stuff knocking about
☀ With no matter around, there's no Friction to slow things down
☀ A complete sucker used in high-tech physics experiments

I'm a riddle. I am what I'm not. A blank space without a crumb of matter. Diddly squat. Ancient scientists thought I was impossible – how could nothing be something? But it's only away from the influence of Mass and matter that the Universe approaches perfection. I cancel out Friction so that Light can travel at its theoretical fastest.

I clean your home, freeze-dry and vacuum-pack food for freshness, and keep your drinks hot or cold in flasks. But step outside your spacecraft in outer space and I'll suck the life out of you in a few minutes. My lack of pressure will also boil your bodily fluids. Astronauts wear pressurized suits to stop this happening. But even in the cold emptiness of space, there's a tiny flicker of restless Energy. You might get something from nothing after all!

Date of discovery: 1643

● Discoverer: Evangelista Torricelli
● Pressure in outer space: 10^{-16} Torr
● Emptiest artificial vacuum: 10^{-13} Torr

Vacuum

Black Body Radiation

■ Hot Stuff

※ A ninja-like shadow who swallows and slays the Light Crew
※ Dark and mysterious, a heat monitor for the Universe
※ The radiation he produces depends only on his heat

I am a master of the dark arts. When an object is pure black like me, it absorbs all the Light that hits it and radiates it back as heat. My special heat "signature" makes me easy to spot and has helped scientists learn about Energy's strange ways. I am the reason why black things heat up and white, shiny objects stay cool.

In hot countries, it's a good idea to wear light colours – black gear may look hip, but it certainly won't keep you cool! I'm not just about gobbling up Energy though – Black Bodies also give off heat much more easily than non-absorbing white or silvery ones. This is why hot things, such as car radiators, get painted black.

Date of discovery: 1862

● Discoverer: Gustav Kirchhoff
● Most unusual Black Bodies (BB): hot stars
● "Best" BB: carbon (absorbs 97% of Light)

Black Body Radiation

Chapter 3

Wave Gang

This small group of movers and shakers create a mighty splash wherever they go. A harmonious bunch, they fill the Universe with Light and Sound as they transport Energy from place to place. The Wave Gang warp space to make this happen, but they don't travel themselves – they just send the Hot Stuff crew along on the wing. Sometimes you can actually see the waves transporting Energy – think of Water Waves or Earthquakes – but other times you only feel the effect of the Energy, such as when a blast of Sound hits you.

Water Wave

Sound

Earthquake

Frequency

Amplitude

Laser

Analogue

Digital

Water Wave

Wave Gang

☀ A totally "rad" method for Energy to travel from A to B
☀ This type of wave uses up-and-down movements
☀ A choppy chap, closely related to Frequency and Amplitude

Aloha! I've never had any qualms about rocking the boat – it's my purpose in life, man. I'm a thrill-seeking surfer-dude who's out to make a few waves! One thing you gotta understand about me is that I ain't going anywhere. I'm just a way for Energy to get around. I only move up and down, like a person in a crowd doing a Mexican wave. No one in the crowd actually moves seats, but the wave (like Energy) travels around the stadium. The more Energy I carry, the higher my peaks.

Surface waves are made by the wind whipping up the water. Deeper water waves are caused by the Moon's Gravity pulling on ocean water. This Energy can be used to generate Electric Current. Dropping in on big swell is bonza, but my talent for seasickness is bogus!

Earliest use of wave power: 1799

● Asian tsunami death toll (2004): 300,000
● Largest Earthquake: N. Sumatra (8.9)
● Height of killer waves: 15 m

Water Wave

Sound
Wave Gang

* Energy waves that are detected by your eardrums
* Travels by vibrations in matter – via "longitudinal" waves
* Can't travel in a Vacuum – no one hears you scream in space!

I surround you – no matter where you go, I'm there, vibrating in your ears. Even the quietest sound moves your eardrum. This is a good thing because it lets you talk with other people and listen to the world's beautiful noises. Kids love loads of me, but older folk tend to like me less and moan about me more.

I get from place to place by causing small disturbances, which are passed along in the same way that shoves and jostles move through a crowd of people. Watch a loudspeaker at work and you'll see how the speaker cone pushes and pulls the air around it. I travel pretty fast, but supersonic jets can "break the sound barrier", releasing huge amounts of Energy in a sonic boom. Thunder is a natural sonic boom.

Sound barrier broken: 1947

● Speed of sound: 330 m/s
● Range of human hearing: 20 – 20,000 Hz
● Loudest sound recorded: Krakatoa (1883)

Sound

Earthquake
Wave Gang

* A sudden release of stored Energy that shakes the ground
* Most of the world's quakes occur in the Pacific "Ring of Fire"
* Tremors are measured on the Richter or Moment Scale

Swift and deadly I hit without warning, spreading mayhem and disaster. I break the Earth like a biscuit, causing landslides, avalanches, fires, mudflows and, of course, tsunamis. Minor quakes often pass harmlessly, but when I come to town I really cause a scene. My seismic waves tear up roads like ribbons and flatten buildings.

I occur when Friction builds up between huge masses of the Earth's crust, about 10 km below the surface. When this stored Energy is released, the crust leaps and buckles. Most of the Energy I generate goes into overcoming Friction. But the rest throws up the ground in a series of waves. P-waves (primary) are compression waves like Sound and travel fastest. S-waves (secondary) are tremors like Water Waves and arrive later.

First Earthquake detector: 132CE

● Quakes per year (over 5.0): 1500
● Biggest quake: Niebla, Chile (1960)
● Deadliest quake: Shaanxi, China (1556)

Earthquake

Frequency
Wave Gang

✳ The amount of repeating wave patterns per unit of time
✳ Related to the pitch of Sound and the Energy of the Light Crew
✳ Measured in Hertz

I'm the most important measure of any wave. I am the one that counts because I tell you how many cycles – or identical patterns of waves – pass a point in a given time. The higher I am, the more peaks and troughs I get through the gate every second. This is measured in Hertz, but – before you ask – no, it doesn't "Hertz"!

Generally speaking, the greater the Frequency, the more Energy waves carry and the straighter line they travel in. This is especially true of the Light Crew. High-frequency Photons can burn and damage cells in your body. Infrasound is low-frequency rumbles, such as whale song, which travel for kilometres. Ultrasound, above the range of human hearing, can boil an egg, but is also used to make scans of babies in the womb.

Earliest use of Hertz: 1930

● Named after: Heinrich Hertz
● 1 Hz = 1 cycle per second
● Mains electricity: 50 Hz

Frequency

Amplitude
Wave Gang

☀ This rowdy hellraiser is a property of all waves
☀ The height of the maximum disturbance in a wave cycle
☀ The more Amplitude a wave has, the more Energy it carries

I love to let my hair down and raise the roof. I'm a party animal and the powerful effects I have on waves keep the neighbourhood awake at night. I'm the measure of a wave's movement – usually taken from its mid point, where the wave is at rest, to the crest – so I can be used to describe any wave you can imagine.

I'm all about agitation and upset. With Water Waves, the higher the wave, the more Energy it carries and the bigger the thrill to ride it. With Sound, increasing me makes the wave louder. When the electromagnetic waves of the Light Crew get just a smidgen more of me, they get brighter. The old codger Analogue uses me to transmit information in waves. He encodes messages into AM Radio Waves by altering the height of the signal.

First AM radio transmission: 1906

● AM inventor: Reginald Fessenden
● Long wave: 153 – 279 kHz
● Medium wave: 520 – 1610 kHz

Amplitude

Laser
Wave Gang

* Fully focused Energy in a fine-tuned light beam
* LASER = Light Amplification by Stimulated Emission of Radiation
* Einstein's idea in 1917; now plays music and stitches up muscles

Highly honed and toned, and at the peak of my game, I make light work of any task! Be it surgery or industrial metalwork, I always cut through to the heart of the matter. Unlike other light sources, I'm totally focused. I use a unique method to whip the waves in my beams into line and keep them tight and under control.

Unlike the rest of the Wave Gang, I've been invented by physicists. I come in all sizes from tiny components in electronic circuit boards to warehouse-sized units for Atom smashing. I'm proud to say I'm spectacularly useful! Not only do I read your CDs and DVDs, I also check bar codes on products, print your documents and protect your valuables. I even undertake tricky eye operations without batting an eyelid!

Earliest known use: 1960

* Inventor: Theodore Maiman
* Max. depth of steel-cutting laser: 6 cm
* Temperature of steel-cutter: 5000 °C

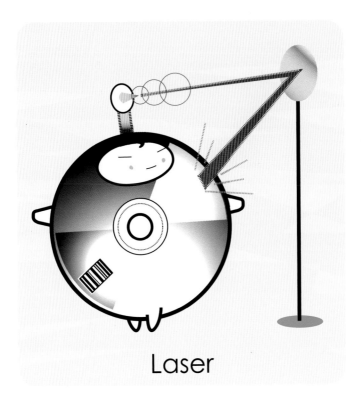

Laser

Analogue
Wave Gang

☀ A way of using "carrier waves" to transmit information
☀ Used for TV and radio broadcasts and old-school sounds
☀ Despite what the purists say, this old fellow is prone to errors

I'm a scratchy old duffer, but I make no apologies. I have had a long and illustrious career in broadcasting, so it feels a little sad as the modern world chooses the fashionable Digital over me. Nevertheless, I prefer to remain a specialist – and I'm not without advantages.

I am the original way of sending information from one place to another, using waves. The trick is to encode information onto "carrier waves", such as Radio Waves or Electric Current. This new, "modulated" wave has peaks and troughs that mirror the original message. It can be decoded to extract the info, but bits of the wave often go missing. My first use was in telephones. Later came radio, TV and vinyl records. Music lovers prefer me to Digital because I'm more faithful to the original sound.

First patented telephone: 1876

● First phone call: Antonio Meucci (1854)
● First radio relay: Mahlon Loomis (1872)
● First LP record: RCA Victor (1930)

Analogue

Digital
Wave Gang

* ☀ An information-encoding method that plays a numbers game
* ☀ Despite its critics, Digital is noise-free, quick and easy
* ☀ Has led to the most incredible explosion of technology

The Digital revolution has happened, my friends! No longer will your music be plagued with horrible hiss! No more will mysterious pings and pops ruin your phone calls! It's all slice-and-dice with me. I'm not prone to errors because I turn info into numbers. You can count on me – after all, I'm just a stream of zeros and ones.

The key to my mastery is sampling. Instead of grafting all the information onto a "carrier wave", like that fuddy-duddy, Analogue, I sample the info at different points. Each point gives you a value that can be encoded as a string of "on" (one) or "off" (zero) signals. This makes the decoder's job much easier and means the info gets through crisply. Which is why I'm used for mobile phones, TVs, computers, CDs, DVDs and satellite systems.

Date of discovery: 1701

● First digital computer: Z3 (1941)
● First comms satellite: SCORE (1958)
● First CD: Philips and Sony (1982)

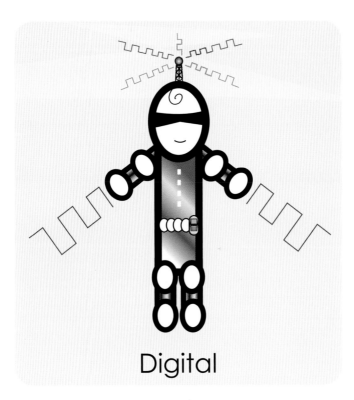

Digital

Chapter 4
Light Crew

This bunch of turbo-charged twinkle-toes are the fastest things in the Universe. Completely massless, they weigh nothing and have the uncanny ability to act like both a particle and a wave. Unlike other waves, however, this bright bunch don't need a material to carry them along. These children of the Sun travel express through the Vacuum of space at the speed of light. Together, the Light Crew make up an electromagnetic spectrum, which means that this colourful crew are essentially all the same – Photons with differing amounts of Energy.

Radio Wave

Microwave

Infrared

Light

Ultraviolet

X-Ray

Gamma Ray

Radio Wave

■ Light Crew

* Old school "wireless" technology, produced in a wide band
* The lowest-frequency member of the Light Crew
* The atmosphere is "invisible" to radio – it sails straight through

I am the workhorse of the airwaves and I'm so useful that governments strictly regulate my use. Made by whipping Electrons up into a frenzy in a thin wire, I am bounced around the world carrying TV and radio transmissions, wireless internet and all your phone calls and texts. Despite the bad press, I'm completely harmless and won't fry your brains when you press your mobile to your sweaty ear.

Sparks and electrical noise interfere with transmitting me cleanly – which is why your radio clicks when you turn on a light – but because I can travel out across space, astronomers go gaga for me. Radio telescopes listen in to the pops and crackles of invisible galaxies, and search for signs of life in the Universe. I'm also used for weather forecasting, spacecraft guidance and radar.

Earliest known use: 1894

● First broadcast: Guglielmo Marconi (1901)
● International Distress Signal (air): 121.5 MHz
● Frequency band: 30 kHz – 300 GHz

Radio Wave

Microwave
■ Light Crew

* High-frequency Radio Waves that have a deep love of water
* Microwaves are produced in devices called "klystrons"
* Gets all sorts of molecules hot under the collar

I'm no ordinary Radio Wave. In fact, I am the top rank of the radio frequency band. With my ability to excite water, fat and sugar molecules, I have single-handedly invented a whole new food industry – the microwave meal! I put molecules in a whirl – when they feel me, they cannot help rotating. As they jostle about, they transfer their motion to each other, increasing the food's internal Kinetic Energy, heating it up.

Microwave ovens are shielded by metal so that I don't cook everything in the kitchen. I'm not that dangerous, just don't try to dry your pets out with me! I'm sneaky too – I'm used by spy satellites and to trap speeding motorists. But stealth bombers are invisible to me, so they fly right under my prying eyes.

Date of discovery: 1888

- Discoverer: Heinrich Hertz
- Microwave oven frequency: 2450 MHz
- Frequency band: 300 MHz – 300 GHz

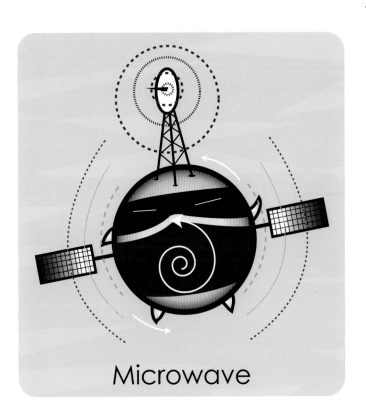

Microwave

Infrared
Light Crew

☀ Hot things give off Infrared, but Infrared isn't the same as heat
☀ Most Infrared from the Sun is blocked by Earth's atmosphere
☀ Remote controls zap your wishes invisibly in Infrared

You can run but you can't hide. I'm the original heatseeker and I'm out to give you a good grilling! Invisible to human eyes, I'm given off by hot things. This makes me an excellent ally if you're in the game of seek-and-destroy. Even in the dark of the night, my telltale signature shines through.

On the battlefield, where targets are often far away, moving fast or hidden, the military lock their missiles on my signal. Night-vision goggles enhance poor light using Infrared, making it easy to spot escaping people. Even some deadly snakes hunt at night using Infrared-vision. But I can also be used to save people. Thermal-imaging cameras are used by rescue services looking for bodies in rubble and by firemen to locate the heart of a blaze.

Earliest known use: World War II

● Average human body temperature: 37 °C
● No. infrared "pit" organs on a snake: 20
● Frequency band: $3 \times 10^5 - 4 \times 10^8$ GHz

Infrared

67

Light
■ Light Crew

☀ Electromagnetic Energy detected by your eyes
☀ White Light is made up of the rainbow spectrum of colours
☀ The light bulb has changed human behaviour patterns forever

Let there be Me! And the world became reality...
I control what the world looks like because I am what
you see when you look at it. You and I have a long
relationship – since most of the Energy coming from
the Sun is in my Frequency band, it is no coincidence
that your eyes have evolved to be sensitive to me.

Plants use my Energy to help them grow, but people
love me so much they have cancelled the night. They
can no longer see the stars in their cities, but their bright
lights can be seen from outer space. Optical fibres now
carry your phone calls, coding your chat into pulses of
Light. Super-speedy optical computers might soon put
Semiconductor out of work, getting the job done in the
blink of an eye. The future's bright – it's blindingly obvious!

Date of discovery: 1670s

● Discoverer: Isaac Newton
● Time to get "night vision": 5 – 10 minutes
● Frequency band: 3.8 – 7.5 x 10^8 GHz

Light

Ultraviolet
Light Crew

✴ Sunburn kings from space, divided into UVA, UVB and UVC
✴ The most energetic Ultraviolet rays can blind you
✴ The Earth's ozone layer stops most of these nasty horrors

We are radiation for Sun worshippers. Eagerly racing from the Sun, there is nothing we love better than fresh bodies laid out on a beach, slathered in coconut oil.

A little of us is a good thing. We lift the clouds and cheer you up if you're feeling down, but a little too much and we start to tinker with the DNA in your cells. We break chemical bonds, unleashing reactive molecules that can cause skin cancers. A pigment in skin called melanin darkens to give more protection against us, but if it wasn't for the ozone layer, we would toast you and turn Earth into a barren desert. We are used in insect zappers and also to sterilize drinking water. Blacklights are UV lights that can spot forged banknotes, make your teeth shine like a crazy fool... and show up your dandruff!

Date of discovery: 1801

● Discoverer: Johann Wilhelm Ritter
● Scorpions glow deadly yellow in UV
● Frequency band: $7.5 \times 10^8 - 3 \times 10^{10}$ GHz

Ultraviolet

X-Ray
■ Light Crew

☀ High-energy radiation that can cause – and cure – cancer
☀ Radiologists wear lead-lined aprons to protect themselves
☀ Exotic and extreme, the "X" actually stands for "unknown"

I am an electromagnetic Peeping Tom, who finds it irresistible to peek inside things. I'm super-keyed up and so exuberant, I can't help slipping inside materials to take a look. Although I'm dangerous company, my talent for spying makes me useful in medicine and industry – I'm a star with that all-important "X" Factor!

I'm made when streams of high-energy Electrons slam into a metal target. My most famous use is in hospitals, where I look for broken bones. I zap straight through soft tissue, but not bones, so they show up as ghostly skeletons on photographic paper. In 1999, the Chandra X-Ray Observatory tuned in on X-Rays from outer space to reveal a scary, unseen Universe, where black holes tear stars apart and neutron stars blow themselves to bits.

Date of discovery: 1895

● Discoverer: Wilhelm Röntgen
● Most powerful X-Ray source: quasars
● Frequency band: $3 \times 10^{10} - 10^{13}$ GHz

X-Ray

Gamma Ray

Light Crew

* A lethal form of nuclear radiation, stopped only by thick lead
* The shortest wavelength and highest-energy Photon
* The main cause of radiation sickness

Fresh from the fire of nuclear reactions, I'll fry you to a crisp. I'm mean, keen and full of beans – I travel at the speed of light and cut right through any material as if it wasn't there. It takes a great thickness of lead to stop me. Because of this, I'm extremely dangerous and can do humans serious damage. Most of the casualties in a nuclear bomb blast are my fault.

Gamma-Ray detectors were put into space in the 1960s to spy for illegal nuclear tests. What they discovered instead were the Universe's most violent explosions – Gamma-Ray bursts. These come from outside our galaxy about once a day, but scientists can't agree on what they are. It's not all about destruction though – I sterilize food and kill off cancer cells… oh, perhaps it is after all!

Date of discovery: 1900

● Discoverer: Paul Villard
● First Gamma-Ray telescope: 1961
● Frequency band: greater than 10^{14} GHz

Gamma Ray

Chapter 5
Atom Family

The Atom Family is a thoroughly modern bunch with many talents. Fun-loving and bouncy, at the last count there were more than 150 of them. What has particle physicists scratching their heads is how they are all related, as some family members can change into other ones. Some are "fundamental particles", which means they cannot be broken down into smaller particles. But all of the Atom Family are very small. Ruled over by the Strong and Weak Forces, weird and surprising things happen to them that are completely out of the ordinary.

Atom

Electron

Proton

Neutron

Quark

Neutrino

Higgs Boson

Strong Force

Antimatter

Atom
Atom Family

* All matter in the Universe is made up of this intriguing chap
* There are 117 different types of Atom known to science
* A stable character with a very long history

I am all around you – every object you pick up or sit on is made of me, even the air you breathe. But I'm so small, you could hide half a million of me behind a single human hair with room to spare. No wonder it took scientists 100 years to track me down!

I am the Big Daddy of the Atom Family. I fit a lot inside me, but mostly I'm empty space. Protons and Neutrons squeeze into my tiny central "nucleus" and Electrons orbit around it. I'm quite happy to lose or share Electrons in chemical reactions with other Atoms. To break me open is easy – you do it every time you switch on the TV – but splitting my nucleus is ridiculously hard and requires loads of Energy. This is why Atoms made at the start of time are still around today. I'm gonna live forever!

Date of discovery: 1803

- Discoverers: John Dalton; Niels Bohr (1913)
- Average size: 1.06×10^{-10} m
- Atomic no. = number of Protons in nucleus

Atom

Electron

Atom Family

☀ Fundamental particle found orbiting an Atom's nucleus
☀ In an Atom there are always as many Electrons as Protons
☀ A feather-light tyke who packs a tremendous punch

I'm a negative particle. Nothing wrong with that. A bit of negativity is healthy. I normally zip around the outer regions of an Atom. I always return and I can't help it – with a negative charge equal to Proton's positive charge, I am constantly drawn towards him. However, you'll never pin me down – I'm so nippy I exist in a blur.

I give Atom his personality but I'm only loosely attached, and I love to buzz off and do my own thing, which often gets me involved in chemical reactions. Life must have been pretty dull before humans learned to use me. In a mere 100 years, I've super-charged the modern world. I make all your electrical gadgets work, from TVs to iPods. I'm also used in electron microscopes. These high-tech snoops can see into the tiny world of the Atom.

Date of discovery: 1897

● Discoverer: J J Thomson
● Group: lepton
● Mass: 9.109×10^{-31} kg

Electron

Proton
■ Atom Family

☀ Subatomic particle found in the nucleus of an Atom
☀ Loves to be at the centre of things
☀ Not a fundamental particle – made up of Quarks

A big, chunky hunk of positivity, I hang out in the centre of an Atom, the nucleus. The nucleus is one of the smallest places imaginable. It's not so great for someone who's as antisocial as me – I can't bear to be around other Protons. However, in spite of the repulsion between us, there I am squished up tight, rammed together by the Strong Force and his Neutron police.

I'm a big fellow, about 2000 times bigger than Electron and just as many times less crazy, so you won't see me shooting all over the place making and breaking alliances. I am much more responsible – I'm what gives Atom his identity. There are 117 different types of Atom, called elements, and they are all unique, thanks to me. Hydrogen is the smallest, with just one Proton.

Date of discovery: 1918

● Discoverer: Ernest Rutherford
● Mass: 1.673×10^{-27} kg
● Made of: 2 "U" Quarks and 1 "D" Quark

Proton

Neutron

■ Atom Family

☀ This fat fellow was the last piece of the atomic jigsaw
☀ Only affected by the Strong Force and Gravity
☀ Made up of Quarks and the key to nuclear chain reactions

No jokes about my size, please. Yes, I am heavy and somewhat stodgy, but I am the glue that holds Atom's nucleus together. Cramped up tightly with Protons, I am a calming influence – without me, the unruly Protons would repel each other and fly off to infinity. Along with the Protons, I beef up Atoms and give them Mass. There are often more Neutrons than Protons in the nucleus, but sometimes a few more of us squeeze in, making heavier (and often radioactive) "isotopes".

My name gives the game away. I am entirely neutral and unaffected by Electromagnetism. Extract me from the nucleus and fire me at the heart of an Atom, and it splits apart. This causes the violent chain reactions that are used in nuclear reactors and atom bombs.

Date of discovery: 1932

● Discoverer: James Chadwick
● Rest Mass: 1.674×10^{-27} kg
● Made of: 1 "U" Quark and 2 "D" Quarks

Neutron

Quark
Atom Family

- A flavoursome bunch of fundamental particles
- Form larger subatomic particles, such as Neutrons and Protons
- "Quark" is not a seagull noise – it actually rhymes with "pork"

Tiny and gentle, we are a gang of six fun-loving fundamental particles. Along with Electrons and Neutrinos, we are basic building blocks of matter, but we exist at an even deeper level, invisible to Light and almost always hidden from detection. We hide in the shadows in the tightest space in the Universe – inside Protons and Neutrons in the nucleus of Atoms.

We come in six different "flavours" called Up, Down, Top, Bottom, Strange and Charm. That may sound to you like we're just missing Dopey to complete the seven dwarfs, but we don't want to hear your wisecracks! We hang out in groups of two or three, and we can swap flavours between us – with the help of the Weak Force. That makes it tough to find out anything solid about us.

Date of discovery: 1964

- Discoverer: Murray Gell-Mann
- Size: 1×10^{-18} m (very largest)
- 2 Quarks = 1 meson; 3 Quarks = 1 baryon

Quark

Neutrino
Atom Family

* Ludicrously slippery fundamental particles in the lepton group
* These energetic particles are produced in nuclear reactions
* Travel close to speed of light and almost impossible to spot

Up, up and away! We are the mavericks of the Atom Family. Trillions upon trillions of us stream off the Sun every second, produced by the nuclear reactions in its core. We move like greased lightning and we're just as slick – almost every single one of us sails clean through the Earth without hitting anything. Over 50 trillion Neutrinos whiz through your body each second, but you don't feel a thing – with almost no Mass and no electrical charge, we're virtually undetectable.

Boffins studying reactions in the Sun use vast vats of dry-cleaning fluid buried in deep mine shafts to watch for us. Tiny puffs of Energy in the liquid signal our passing. It took 26 years to find us: in theory, we come in three "flavours", but so far, only one has been spotted.

Date of discovery: 1956

● Discoverers: Wolfgang Pauli; Reines & Cowan
● Named by: Enrico Fermi
● Mass: currently too small to measure

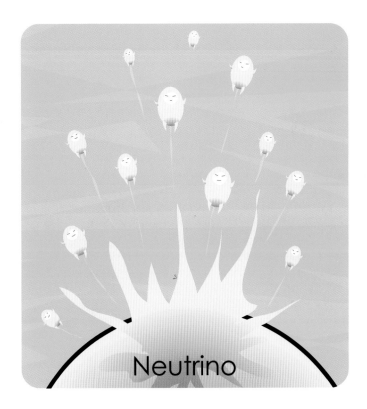

Neutrino

Higgs Boson
■ Atom Family

☀ Thought to be the particle that gives Mass to matter
☀ The subject of physics' greatest manhunt
☀ No one's certain that this little fella exists at all

Extremely shy and retiring, I've played hide and seek with the greatest minds in physics for more than 40 years. I'm the one that got away! Theoretical scientists are desperate to find me because I am the missing link in all their theories about matter.

They reckon I cluster around particles of matter, giving them Mass. It's funny how something as unobtrusive as me could give Mass to anything, but this idea explains where Mass comes from and why it's always positive. Physicists also think that I might be the reason why there's more matter than Antimatter in the Universe. They are so keen to find me, they've built a hugely expensive, 27 km-long Proton-smashing machine, called the Large Hadron Collider (LHC), in Geneva, Switzerland. The hunt is on!

As yet unobserved

● Proposed by: Peter Higgs
● AKA: the "God particle"
● Energy of LHC beam: 350 MJ

Higgs Boson

Strong Force

■ Atom Family

✳ The force of attraction that holds the Atom's nucleus together
✳ The strongest of the four fundamental forces
✳ Responsible for nasty Radioactivity, such as Alpha Particles

I am the Universe's strongman. The Magnificent!
The Unbeatable! I am over 100 times stronger than
Electromagnetism and a million times stronger than
the Weak Force, and without me there'd be no Atoms.

Inside an Atom's nucleus a tremendous battle is going
on between me and the force of Electromagnetism.
He makes positively charged Protons repel each other
violently, but I slave tirelessly to keep it all together –
without me, they would hurtle off into infinity. My special
interaction makes Protons attractive to one another, but
it only works over very small distances. It's really difficult
to hold together the nucleus of big Atoms and sometimes
it gets too much. When my powers break down, the
nucleus splits, releasing radioactive Alpha Particles.

Date of discovery: 1934

● Discoverer: Hideki Yukawa
● Range: 10^{-15} m
● Carrier: gluon particle

Strong Force

Antimatter
Atom Family

* Antimatter is the opposite of normal matter
* Antiparticles have all their properties reversed, except Mass
* The world's most expensive stuff and a potential superfuel

Did you think I was mere science fiction? Think again!
I'm science fact, baby, and you'd better get wise to
me! I am matter's evil twin and the nemesis of every
Atom in your body. When my dark, mirror-image (anti)
particles come into contact with particles of matter, we
mutually destroy each other in a flash of raw Energy.

All of my Mass is transferred instantly into super-energetic
Gamma Rays – a return on investment unheard of in the
Energy generation game, making me about 10 billion
times more powerful than burning oil. A half-gram of me
would be enough to set off a Hiroshima-sized blast. I am
just the ticket to power spacecraft to the stars, but I'm
fiendishly hard to produce, and with a track record for
destruction of matter, I'm devilishly tricky to store.

Date of discovery: 1927

● Discoverers: Paul Dirac; CERN (1995)
● Amount made per year: 0.000000005 g
● Cost per milligram: £150 billion

Antimatter

Chapter 6

Nuclear Heavies

You wouldn't think that these tiny fellows could pack such a punch, but this bunch of heavy-hitters can do a lot of damage. Renegades expelled from the wreckage of heavy Atoms as their nuclei break apart, the Nuclear Heavies wreak havoc wherever they go. They burn skin, cause cancers and trigger nuclear bomb blasts – in short, things get nasty fast when these troublemakers turn up. But it's mainly thanks to these quantum thugs that we know loads about the weird life of the Atom Family. They truly are to die for!

Radioactivity

Alpha Particle

Beta Particle

Photon

Schrödinger's Cat

Weak Force

Radioactivity
Nuclear Heavies

- ✸ I'm what happens when Atoms break down
- ✸ An unpleasant character used to date ancient artifacts
- ✸ Detected by a Geiger counter and measured in Becquerels

Handle me with care – I'm well-known to be touchy and temperamental. Like a sickness, I affect Atoms that have more than 83 Protons in the nucleus. I am the offspring of a titanic battle between Electromagnetism and the Strong Force, which causes the nuclei of heavy Atoms to split apart. This atomic temper tantrum spits out sprays of Alpha and Beta Particles, and bursts of Gamma Rays.

Before I was properly understood, I killed many scientists, but I can be put to good use. I am used in nuclear power stations, and I also sterilize food and kill cancer cells. My level of activity is measured by the length of my "half life" – the time it takes me to break down half of the Atoms in a thing. I hang about for ages – this is why toxic nuclear waste oozes into soil and poisons water for years.

Date of discovery: 1896

- ● Discoverer: Henri Becquerel
- ● Half-life of uranium-235: 700 million years
- ● Worst nuclear accident: Chernobyl (1986)

Radioactivity

Alpha Particle
Nuclear Heavies

* The biggest particle of nuclear radiation
* Slow-moving and heavy, and incredibly destructive
* Can be stopped by a thin sheet of paper

As far as things go in the teeny-tiny world of sub-atomic particles, I am a big, ugly bruiser. I'm as chunky as a helium atom nucleus (in fact, that's what I really am). In short, I'm not to be messed with – better steer clear of me.

I have a mean streak as wide as the Grand Canyon. When I get into your body, I plough into Atoms, wreaking havoc with your cells and causing cancers. Luckily for you, just a few layers of skin is enough to stop me getting inside. Unlucky though for the Russian journalist Alexander Litvinenko, whom I killed in 2006, after he was fed the alpha-particle-emitting isotope polonium-210.

Smokers beware – I'm found in cigarettes but, as a vital component of smoke detectors, I could save your life too.

Date of discovery: 1898

● Discoverer: Ernest Rutherford
● Weight: 6.644656×10^{-27} kg
● Made of: 2 Protons, 2 Neutrons

Alpha Particle

Beta Particle
Nuclear Heavies

☀ This vivacious dude is a fast-moving particle of nuclear radiation
☀ A negative "free" Electron, stopped by a thin sheet of metal
☀ More than 7000 times lighter than Alpha Particle

I burst out of a decaying radioactive Atom's nucleus like a bat out of hell. I've got places to go and I don't want to hang around! But I need help to escape from an overcrowded nucleus. My good friend the Weak Force makes a Neutron change into a Proton, which creates me in the process, and I'm outta there!

I am so much smaller and lighter than Alpha Particles, I can zip through materials more easily. This makes me very dangerous for humans. I'll travel right through your skin and can damage the DNA in your body's cells. I'm used for finding leaks in pipes, controlling thickness in paper and sheet metal production, and to sterilize food. In medicine, I'm used as a "tracer" to track the body's inner workings and make 3D scans of it.

Date of discovery: 1896

● Discoverer: Henri Becquerel
● Mass: 9.109×10^{-31} kg
● Common medical tracer: strontium-90

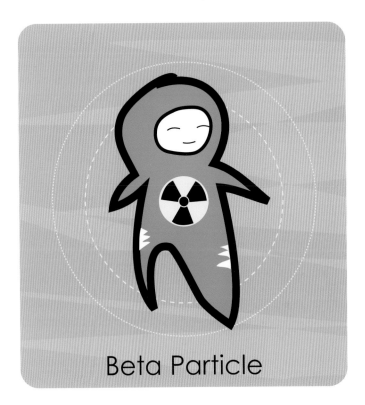

Beta Particle

Photon
■ Nuclear Heavies

* A real livewire who brings sparkle and fizz wherever he goes
* The Light Crew are all made from this little guy
* Spat out of radioactive nuclei as high-energy Gamma Rays

I am simply the fastest thing in the Universe. I have no Mass, so I whiz along at the speed of light. I have bamboozled physicists for years with my ability to act like a particle one second and a wave the next.

I'm also the hardest worker in the Universe – I speed between the Sun and Earth in continuous streams, bounce off mirrors so that you can see reflections and carry the electromagnetic force around. I die when I interact with anything and I leap into existence when anything gets overexcited. After my job is done, I'm re-absorbed – after all, I'm only a blip of Energy. I bring Light to the world, but your eyes need to collect about a hundred Photons to detect it. I expose photographic films, fade your clothes and also make solar cells work.

Date of discovery: 1905

● Discoverer: Albert Einstein
● Mass: 0 kg
● Photon acts as both wave and particle

Photon

Schrödinger's Cat

Nuclear Heavies

✳ The subject of a famous cat-astrophic thought experiment
✳ A freaky feline who helps boffins understand the quantum world
✳ The purr-fect proof that reality is not simple

I was dreamt up by Erwin Schrödinger, and since then I've been living in a box, neither alive nor dead. Let me explain: in the world of subatomic particles incredibly weird things go on that don't happen in the everyday world. These "quantum" effects make sure that particles only have properties, such as Speed, when they are observed. Erwin was trying to figure out what this meant for more fun things, such as cats. He asked scientists to imagine me shut in a box with a radioactive source. If the source decays, it releases poison gas from a bottle and I kick the bucket. If not, I stay alive! But until someone looks in the box the source has neither decayed nor not decayed – so I am neither alive nor dead!

Date of discovery: 1935

● Chance of Alpha decay: 50%
● Deadly gas: Hydrocyanic acid
● No one has ever tried this experiment

Schrödinger's Cat

Weak Force
Nuclear Heavies

* The force of attraction between Quarks, Electrons and Neutrinos
* A fundamental force that changes the flavour of Quarks
* Teams up with the Strong Force in extreme conditions

I have to be honest with you, I'm a little upset to be known as the Weak Force. I'm no weakling – I'm over a billion trillion trillion times stronger than Gravity! OK, so I am thousands of times weaker than Electromagnetism, but since I battle with feisty Protons in the titchy confines of an Atom's nucleus, you can hardly call me a wimp!

I only work over tiny distances, but I have big-time effects. Without my force the Sun wouldn't shine. At the crucial point in the fusion reaction in the Sun's core, I work my magic on the Quarks in a Proton, which changes into a Neutron. This releases trillions of Neutrinos, which pour out of the Sun and stop the reaction grinding to a halt. I can also change Neutrons into Protons in unstable Atoms, a trick that releases a radioactive Beta Particle.

Date of discovery: 1957

● Discoverers: Glashow, Salam & Weinberg
● Range: about 10^{-18} m
● Carriers: W, W+ and Z particles

Weak Force

Chapter 7
Electric Cuties

Danger! High Voltage! Don't be fooled – the Electric Cuties aren't quite the darling dears they'd have you believe. Electricity is a form of Energy – misuse it and this lot will punish you hard. Sparks always fly when these twisted devils get together. They are also shockingly hip. The undisputed masters of modernity, they are in charge of running every electronic gadget in the world, as well as generating electricity. The beating heart of this gang and the source of their amazing powers is Electromagnetism – a fundamental force of nature.

Static Electricity

Electric Current

Magnetism

Electromagnetism

Generator

Semiconductor

Static Electricity
■ Electric Cuties

☀ Electrical charge that stays in one place
☀ This hair-raising character causes lightning
☀ A bright spark who'll give you a real charge

People say I'm a useless nuisance. I like to mooch about on the surface of things, going nowhere fast. But I'm full of surprises – I provide the crackle when you take off your jumper and I'll give you a little shock just to remind you I'm there! I may not be as dynamic as Electric Current but don't think I'm lazy. When I move, I'm gone in a flash. As lightning, I kill about 1000 people per year.

I'm caused when two electrical insulators rub together. Electrons get scraped off one surface and put onto the other, leaving each surface with the opposite electrical charge. My irresistible attraction to opposite charges is used in inkjet printers and photocopiers to pull electrically charged ink onto the paper. I also control the flow of current in most electronic circuits.

Date of discovery: 600BCE

● Typical lightning current: 10,000 amps
● Typical lightning voltage: 100 million volts
● Typical lightning temperature: 30,000 °C

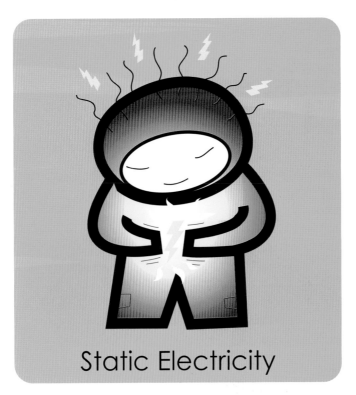

Static Electricity

Electric Current

■ Electric Cuties

☀ A form of Energy carried by moving electrical charges
☀ "Jump-started" by a famous frog's-leg experiment
☀ A shocking phenomenon, measured in amps

I'm nothing like my layabout brother Static Electricity. My Electrons like to go with the flow and, with their help, I light up the world. No question, I'm the man of the last 200 years. Without me there would be no TV, phones or computers – life would be pretty dull because there wouldn't even be electric light bulbs!

As a sparky form of Energy, I can be turned into Light, Sound or motion, but I need a complete circuit to work. The chemical Potential Energy in batteries provides the "push" to move Electrons around. But although I zap around circuits in the blink of an eye, the Electrons actually move very slowly. You've got to be careful if I'm about – I mess with the Atoms in your body when you get a shock and I'm a very cruel way to kill people.

Date of discovery: 1799

● Discoverer: Alessandro Volta
● Speed of electrons in a wire: 0.1 mm/s
● Lethal current: 5 – 8 amps

Electric Current

Magnetism
Electric Cuties

- ☀ An invisible force caused only by certain solids and fluids
- ☀ Magnets have north and south poles that attract each other
- ☀ Neither of Earth's magnetic poles is at the geographic pole

I may not be a fundamental force, but I'm not useless. I'm bi-polar with a strong north-south divide. Sprinkle iron filings near me and you'll see that I'm surrounded by an invisible forcefield, which gets its power from my Atoms. The spin of their Electrons makes every one slightly magnetic, but the effect becomes noticeable only when billions of them line up in the same direction.

I'm an integral part of the Earth – use me to get your bearings with a compass. I also protect you from deadly cosmic rays. Cassettes and videos once used strips of magnetic tape to record information, but now people prefer Laser technology. I am found in computer hard drives, bank cards and security tags. The magnets in hospital MRI machines can rip a watch off your arm.

Earliest known use: 2BCE

- ● North pole (estimate): 82.7° N 114.4° W
- ● South pole (estimate): 63.5° S 138.0° E
- ● Shifting of magnetic poles: 40 km/year

Magnetism

Electromagnetism

■ Electric Cuties

- ☀ Attraction and repulsion between electrically charged objects
- ☀ The second-strongest fundamental force, but the most useful
- ☀ A helpful fellow carried from place to place by the Light Crew

Forget anything written by those two circus clowns, the Weak and Strong Forces! No doubt they've been filling your head with their hot air about how powerful they are. Welcome to the real world! Gravity and I are the only forces that matter outside the ridiculously tiny distances of the atomic nucleus. You actually *feel* us.

I'm the rule that opposites attract. I cause attraction between opposite-charged particles and repulsion between like-charged particles. I keep Electrons happy hanging around Atoms, get Electric Currents moving and allow matter to hold its shape. I stop you sinking through your chair and your hand from going through this book. I'm the dream-team combo of electric and magnetic fields and I get around at the speed of light.

Date of discovery: 1820

- ● Discoverer: Hans Christian Oersted
- ● Range: infinite
- ● Carrier: Photon

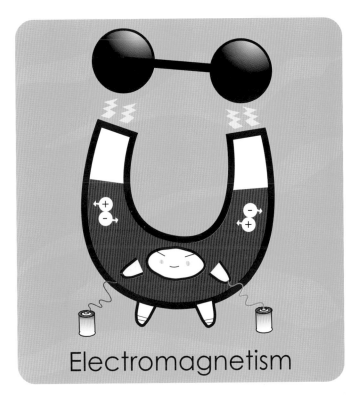

Electromagnetism

Generator
■ Electric Cuties

☀ A dynamic dervish who generates electricity
☀ Uses Electromagnetism to supply us with Energy
☀ Powers houses and industry, runs trains and recharges batteries

Cool, calm and collected, I'm the backbone of the modern world. Ultimately, all your energy needs are met by me. Quiet and unassuming I do my work behind the scenes, but with dash and panache, if I may say so.

My flair is for "magicking" electricity out of thin air using Electromagnetism. It's simplicity itself. Spin a coil of wire inside a magnetic field and the Electrons in the wire get up on their toes and move – you have yourself an Electric Current. (The generators used in power stations actually spin electromagnets inside huge coils of wire.) The secret of my success is that the fundamental electromagnetic force is made up of magnetic and electric fields. If only one field is there, Electromagnetism has the knack of automatically generating the other.

Date of discovery: 1831

● Discoverer: Michael Faraday
● First generator: Hippolyte Pixii (1832)
● Output of largest power station: 18.2 GW

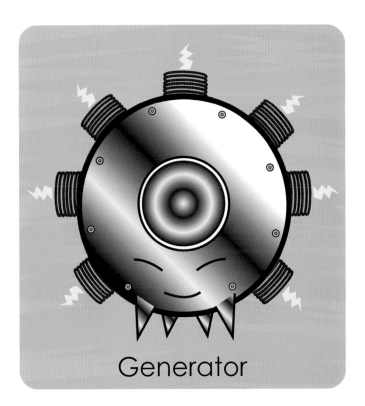

Generator

Semiconductor

Electric Cuties

☀ Strange materials that don't really like to conduct electricity
☀ Every Digital device is jam-packed with this clever fellow
☀ A logical genius and star of the show in computers

I'm a technological wizard. I "conduct" affairs in every piece of electronic equipment, telling Electric Current where to go and how to act. The funny thing is, I'm not terribly good at conducting electricity, but I've made my vice a virtue.

I'm made using chemical elements known as semi-metals – strange materials that don't quite know whether they are metals or non-metals. But I can't perform unless I've had some impurities added first. This "doping" lets Electric Current flow, but only in certain directions, which is key to my fantastic usefulness. When Semiconductor "sandwiches" are laid down in microchips, it allows all kinds of complicated logic decisions and makes me the brains of the computer.

Date of discovery: 1947

● Discoverer: Bell Laboratories
● Common materials: silicon, germanium
● Industry value: £100 billion per year

Semiconductor

Index

Glossary

Antiparticle A subatomic particle with the same Mass as a particle of normal matter, but with opposite properties. Antimatter is made up of Antiparticles.

Baryon A subatomic particle made of three Quarks. Protons and Neutrons are baryons.

Black hole The densest thing in the Universe. So massive that not even Light can escape its Gravity.

Carrier wave A wave that is modulated, or "tuned" to carry information. FM and AM are ways of modulating Radio Waves to send information.

Chain reaction A nucleus-splitting atomic reaction that quickly snowballs. Used in nuclear reactors and Atom bombs.

Doping Adding impurities to an electrical non-conducting material to make it a Semiconductor.

Fission Splitting the nucleus of heavy Atoms.

Forcefield The area where one object feels a Force from another object (e.g. gravitational attraction).

Fundamental force One of four crucial interactions that govern how the Universe works. Electromagnetism and Gravity are long-range; the Strong and Weak Forces are short-range.

Fundamental particle The most basic bit of matter – a particle that can't be split into smaller, simpler bits.

Fusion Joining together the nuclei of light Atoms.

Isotope Atoms of the same element that have the same number of Protons but differing amounts of Neutrons. Heavy isotopes are often radioactive.

Lepton A small fundamental particle affected by the Weak Force. Electrons and Neutrinos are leptons.

Meson A subatomic particle made of two Quarks.

Nucleus The heart of an Atom, composed of Protons and Neutrons.

Quantum theory A strange branch of physics that shows how Light can act like a particle and Electrons and other particles have wave-like properties.

Glossary

Radiation sickness Damage to DNA in the cells of the body caused by Alpha and Beta Particles, Gamma Rays and Neutrons. Can be lethal.

Radioactive dating A way of dating rocks, fossils, bones and other ancient stuff by calculating the number of radioactive Atoms that have decayed.

Ring of Fire A "circle" of intense Earthquake activity around the edges of the Pacific Ocean, caused by the movement of the Earth's tectonic plates.

Sonic boom A "thunderclap" when the shockwave from a plane breaking the sound barrier – travelling faster than the speed of Sound – touches the ground.

Subatomic Anything smaller than the Atom.

Thought experiment An imaginary scenario dreamt up by a scientist to test out a theory.

Tracer A radioactive substance, put inside the body to track the workings of the internal organs.

Zero-point Energy The lowest possible energy.